NEW ZEALAND

ABDO
Publishing Company

NEW ZEALAND

by Rebecca Hirsch

Content Consultant
Alan C. Tidwell
Director of the Center for Australian and New Zealand Studies
Georgetown University

CREDITS

Published by ABDO Publishing Company, PO Box 398166, Minneapolis, MN 55439. Copyright © 2013 by Abdo Consulting Group, Inc. International copyrights reserved in all countries. No part of this book may be reproduced in any form without written permission from the publisher. The Essential Library™ is a trademark and logo of ABDO Publishing Company.

Printed in the United States of America,
North Mankato, Minnesota
092012
012013

THIS BOOK CONTAINS AT LEAST 10% RECYCLED MATERIALS.

Editor: Arnold Ringstad
Series Designer: Emily Love

About the Author: Rebecca Hirsch, PhD, is a former molecular biologist who now writes for children and teens. She has written more than 20 books on geography, science, and the environment. She writes from her home in State College, Pennsylvania, where she lives with her husband and three children.

Cataloging-in-Publication Data

Hirsch, Rebecca.
 New Zealand / Rebecca Hirsch.
   p. cm. -- (Countries of the world)
Includes bibliographical references and index.
ISBN 978-1-61783-631-2
1. New Zealand--Juvenile literature.   I. Title.
993--dc22

2012946077

Cover: New Zealand's Banks Peninsula

TABLE OF CONTENTS

CHAPTER 1

A VISIT TO NEW ZEALAND

As the tour bus winds through snow-topped mountains, you shift uncomfortably in your seat. You have heard this road is one of the most avalanche prone in the world. Through the bus window, a mountain looms ahead, a rough-hewn tunnel at its base. The bus enters the tunnel. The passage is narrow, steep, and dark. You emerge into the sunlight on the other side and begin your descent into a green valley. Through the trees, you catch glimpses of sheer rock walls. Finally, the bus turns into a parking lot and rolls to a stop. As you step off the bus, the driver smiles and calls out after you, "Welcome to Milford Sound, mate."

With so many indentations, New Zealand's coastline is longer than China's.

Milford Sound is surrounded by steep mountains.

A LAND OF BEAUTY AND ADVENTURE

New Zealand may be small, but it packs a lot of variety into a compact space. Its landscapes are so otherworldly the country was chosen as a stand-in for the mythical realm Middle Earth during the filming of the *Lord of the Rings* movies. You may find yourself hiking—trekking or tramping, as New Zealanders call it—in a mossy forest, surrounded by tree ferns, vines, and palms. Round a bend, and suddenly you are staring at a snow-capped peak or a plunging waterfall or the sparkling sea.

New Zealand is roughly the size of Colorado.

Wilderness is never far away in New Zealand. A third of the country is protected within national parks and preserves.[1] In these areas, you can see cloud-piercing volcanoes, enormous glaciers, rocky mountains, rolling hillsides, lush rain forests, and mile after mile of sun-drenched beaches.

Milford Sound is located in one of the wildest parts of New Zealand. The best way to experience Milford Sound is by boat, so as soon as you arrive, you head for the water. An hour later, you are paddling a kayak past steep mountains rising out of the water on all sides. Trees cling to the rocky slopes. You have heard that sometimes there are tree avalanches here, when trees lose their grip on the mountain and slide into the water. You paddle around a corner and come upon a thundering waterfall pouring down the sheer rock face.

With such varied scenery, New Zealand has become known as a thrill-seeker's paradise. The land invites outdoor activities. The climate is mild, the landscape diverse, and the ocean usually not more than an hour away. There are lakes and rivers for kayaking, rocks for climbing, beaches for surfing, and trails for mountain biking. You can also ski, snowboard, bungee jump, golf, or skydive. If you prefer the water, you can go whale watching, jet boating, or white-water rafting. But there is more to New Zealand than adventure and striking landscapes.

BUNGEE JUMPING

New Zealander A. J. Hackett helped popularize bungee jumping in 1988 when he strapped rubber cords to his ankles and leaped off a historic bridge in Queenstown. Today, bungee jumping is one of New Zealand's most popular daredevil pursuits. Jumping is actually quite safe, and operators are highly trained to reduce the inherent risks of leaping off a bridge or hurtling into a gorge.

TWO CULTURES

The next day, you venture into Christchurch, the largest city on South Island. Along with North Island, this is one of the two major islands that make up New Zealand. You stroll along the picturesque Avon River, which threads through the city. Kiwis, as New Zealanders call themselves,

lounge in the grass beside the river. Other people bicycle along the shore. A man stands at one end of a long, flat-bottomed boat, pushing it along with a pole. Christchurch is lush, green, and picturesque. It has also been called the most British city outside of the United Kingdom.

A British colony for many years, New Zealand is now independent and a member of the British Commonwealth. Although British flavor still pervades everyday life, New Zealand has come into its own as an independent nation. It has emerged as a social democracy where civil rights are protected and women hold important political offices.

The society is solidly bicultural; New Zealand recognizes and celebrates its native people, the Maori. The country has two official languages, English and Maori. But there is a balancing act between the two cultures, and New Zealand still struggles with inequality.

THE PARADOX OF NEW ZEALAND

As you get to know this country, you discover New Zealand's short but rich history, its lively cities, and its reputation as a leader in human rights. You also meet people known for their friendly spirit and keen sense of

New Zealand Sign Language (NZSL) is used by more than 20,000 people in New Zealand.

Visitors tour a Maori meetinghouse in the city of Rotorua.

THE BRITISH COMMONWEALTH

At its height in the late nineteenth century, the British Empire covered almost one-fourth of the world's land area and contained more than one-fourth of its population. But in the early decades of the twentieth century, many of its possessions around the globe asserted their independence. As a result, the empire slowly morphed into the British Commonwealth, a group of nations that are independent but still pledge symbolic allegiance to the British monarch. The founding members in 1931 were the United Kingdom, New Zealand, Australia, Canada, and South Africa. Over time, the Commonwealth swelled to include more than 50 member nations. Though Commonwealth membership includes no formal obligations, members are joined by shared traditions and experiences.

adventure. These are, after all, the people who popularized the sport of bungee jumping.

New Zealand's past has given birth to a paradoxical nature. As a former British colony, it can feel like a slice of Britain, yet it sits far from the United Kingdom in the South Pacific Ocean. It prides itself on being a model for civil rights, yet among some Maori, resentments over injustices linger. It is renowned for its unusual wildlife, yet an astonishing number of species have disappeared in less than one millennium of human habitation. It has a

The Avon River winds through the busy city of Christchurch.

New Zealand is a land of striking landscapes
and wildlife.

reputation for being clean and green, yet people have had a profound and
rapid impact on the land.

Kiwis are curious and friendly toward visitors. They like to ask,
"How do you like New Zealand?" New Zealanders take pride in the

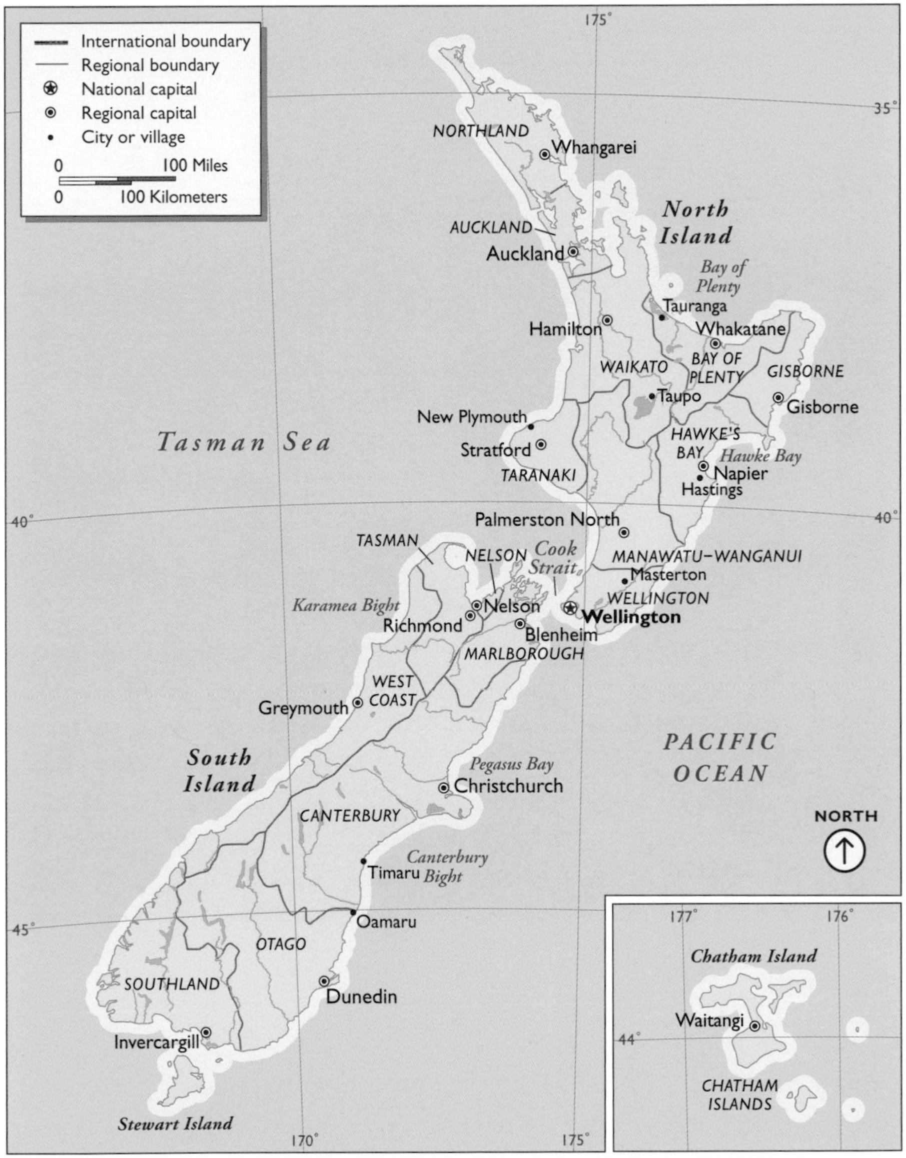
International boundary
Regional boundary
National capital
Regional capital
City or village
0 100 Miles
0 100 Kilometers
175°
35°
40°
45°
170°
NORTHLAND
Whangarei
North Island
AUCKLAND
Auckland
Bay of Plenty
Tauranga
Hamilton
Whakatane
WAIKATO
BAY OF PLENTY
GISBORNE
Taupo
Gisborne
New Plymouth
Tasman Sea
Stratford
HAWKE'S BAY
Hawke Bay
TARANAKI
Napier
Hastings
Palmerston North
TASMAN
NELSON
Cook Strait
MANAWATU–WANGANUI
Masterton
WELLINGTON
Karamea Bight
Nelson
Richmond
Wellington
Blenheim
MARLBOROUGH
WEST COAST
Greymouth
PACIFIC OCEAN
South Island
Pegasus Bay
Christchurch
CANTERBURY
NORTH
Canterbury Bight
Timaru
Oamaru
OTAGO
SOUTHLAND
Dunedin
Invercargill
Stewart Island
177°
176°
Chatham Island
Waitangi
44°
CHATHAM ISLANDS

Political Boundaries of New Zealand

New Zealanders are proud of their country's scenic landscapes.

natural beauty of their land. They even call it Godzone, meaning "God's own country."

SNAPSHOT

Official name: New Zealand

Capital city: Wellington

Form of government: parliamentary democracy

Title of leaders: prime minister (head of government); king or queen (head of state)

Currency: New Zealand dollar

Population (July 2012 est.): 4,327,944
World rank: 126

Size: 103,363 square miles (267,710 square km)
World rank: 76

Language: English, Maori

Official religion: none

Per capita GDP (2011, US dollars): $27,900
World rank: 48

CHAPTER 2

GEOGRAPHY: VARIETY IN A SMALL SPACE

The first people to arrive in New Zealand called it Aotearoa, or "the land of the long white cloud." European explorers named the long, thin, and sparsely populated island nation New Zealand in the seventeenth century. The country is among the largest oceanic archipelagos on the planet.

New Zealand is located approximately 990 miles (1,600 km) southeast of Australia. Its three main islands are North Island, South Island, and the much smaller Stewart Island. More than 700 relatively tiny islands dot the waters off the coasts. The narrow Cook Strait separates North Island and South Island. The smaller Stewart Island lies just south of South Island. All together, New Zealand covers 103,363 square miles (267,710 sq km).[1]

Auckland, set between water and rolling hills, is the largest city in New Zealand.

Most New Zealanders live on North Island and South Island. North Island features Auckland, New Zealand's largest city, as well as the capital city of Wellington. South Island has fewer people, the city of Christchurch, and more wilderness.

New Zealand is divided into 16 regions: nine on North Island and seven on South Island. Borders between regions are generally drawn along natural divisions, such as mountain ranges or the lines between neighboring drainage basins. The most populous region, Auckland, holds approximately 1.5 million people. The least populous, the West Coast region of South Island, contains just under 32,000.[2] The largest region by land area is Canterbury on South Island, which encompasses more than 16,000 square miles (42,000 sq km).[3] The smallest is Nelson, also on South Island, at only 170 square miles (440 sq km).[4]

The land has been shaped by its location in the Pacific Ring of Fire, an area with a large number of earthquakes and volcanoes. The islands sit over the edges of two tectonic plates: the Indo-Australian

SUNSHINE IN NEW ZEALAND

New Zealand lies just west of the international date line, which means it is the first country to see the sunrise every day. The island nation is famous for its sunshine. Much of the country receives 2,000 hours of sunshine a year, and some places bask in the sun even more. One of the sunniest spots is the city of Nelson, which in 2010 received more than 2,570 hours of sunshine.[5] Because New Zealand sees so much sunlight, the country has high rates of melanoma, a type of skin cancer.

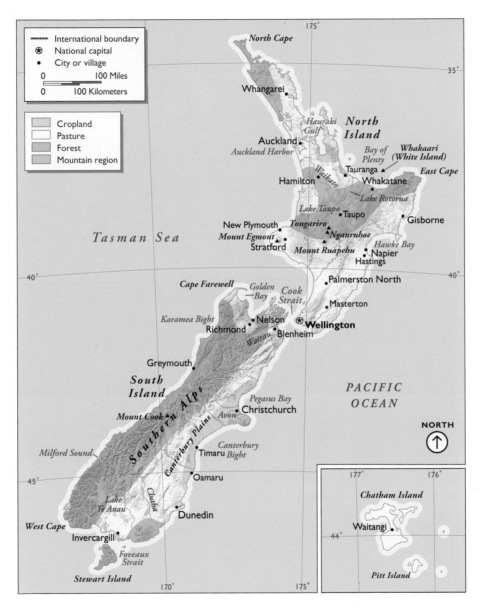

Geography of New Zealand

Map legend:
- International boundary
- National capital
- City or village

0 — 100 Miles
0 — 100 Kilometers

- Cropland
- Pasture
- Forest
- Mountain region

North Cape
Whangarei
Hauraki Gulf
North Island
Auckland
Auckland Harbor
Waikato
Bay of Plenty
Whakaari (White Island)
Hamilton
Tauranga
Whakatane
East Cape
Lake Taupo
Lake Rotorua
New Plymouth
Taupo
Gisborne
Tongariro
Mount Egmont
Ngauruhoe
Stratford
Mount Ruapehu
Hawke Bay
Napier
Hastings
Palmerston North
Tasman Sea
Cape Farewell
Golden Bay
Cook Strait
Masterton
Karamea Bight
Nelson
Wellington
Richmond
Wairau
Blenheim
Greymouth
South Island
Southern Alps
Pegasus Bay
Christchurch
Mount Cook
Avon
Canterbury Plains
PACIFIC OCEAN
Milford Sound
Canterbury Bight
Timaru
NORTH ↑
Oamaru
Chatham Island
Lake Te Anau
Clutha
Waitangi
West Cape
Dunedin
Invercargill
Foveaux Strait
Pitt Island
Stewart Island

Living next to a large, active volcano such as
Mount Ruapehu can be dangerous.

Plate and the Pacific Plate. Collisions of these plates over millions of
years have shaped the land in powerful ways, giving rise to New Zealand's
high mountains, majestic volcanoes, and deep lakes. Earthquakes and
volcanic eruptions remain a danger.

MOUNTAINS AND VOLCANOES

North Island consists mostly of rolling hills covered by farmland. Narrow mountain ranges stretch along the southern part of the island, many peaking at more than 4,900 feet (1,500 m).[6] In the center of the island, volcanoes rise up near Lake Taupo, the country's largest lake. Nearby, pools of mud boil and geysers erupt, more signs of volcanic activity.

Three large volcanoes in the central area of North Island are still active. The largest and most active is Mount Ruapehu. When this snow-capped volcano erupts, steam and ash explode out of the top and melt the snow. This forms lahars, volcanic mudflows that stream down well-worn tracks on the mountainside. Mount Ruapehu last erupted at 8:26 p.m. on September 25, 2007, producing lahars and showering the summit with rock and ash. The eruption caused no fatalities but reminded New Zealanders of the risk of living near volcanoes.

South Island is mountainous. The Southern Alps stretch hundreds of miles north to south along the island, rising to more than 12,000 feet (3,600 m).[7] The collision of tectonic plates pushed the Earth's crust upward, creating the mountain range. To the west of the mountains are rain forests, and to the east sits a large coastal plain that is mostly farmland. Lying just 17 miles (27 km) south of South Island, Stewart Island is made up of rolling hills covered with native vegetation.[8]

GLACIERS AND FJORDS

Twenty thousand years ago, Earth was cooler. Massive ice sheets called glaciers lay over much of New Zealand. Under pressure from the weight of the ice above, the glaciers flowed from the mountains to the low-lying areas. As they flowed, they shaped the land, carving out steep valleys and carrying rocky debris from the mountains to the low-lying areas.

Because so much of Earth's water was locked inside glaciers, sea levels dropped. When the world warmed and the glaciers melted, water filled the valleys, creating deep lakes. Sea levels rose, and water rushed into the carved-out valleys near the sea. The mounds of debris that had been swept down by the glaciers formed natural dams and partially blocked the inrushing sea. This process created a series of deep fjords—long, narrow inlets of the sea surrounded by high cliffs. These fjords form long fingers along the southwestern part of South Island's coastline.

Fiordland National Park stretches across 3 million acres (1.2 million ha) and encompasses lakes, mountain peaks, and deep

fjords. Along the West Coast of South Island, glaciers still flow from the Southern Alps. The steepest and fastest moving is Franz Josef Glacier.

LAKES, RIVERS, AND COASTS

There are many lakes in New Zealand. North Island's lakes were largely formed by volcanoes, while glaciers were responsible for many of the lakes on South Island. New Zealand's lakes are used for fishing, boating, and drinking water. The largest of these lakes is North Island's Lake Taupo, which covers 234 square miles (606 sq km).[9] It sits in the deep basin of a volcano that erupted thousands of years ago.

New Zealand's longest river is the Waikato on North Island. It begins on the slopes of Mount Ruapehu and drains into Lake Taupo before flowing out of the lake and passing through several hydroelectric dams on its way to the Pacific Ocean. Many other rivers flow from New Zealand's highlands to the coast. These rivers tend to be short and fast moving. They are used for fishing, drinking water, and irrigation.

The long, thin North and South Islands have coastlines that twist and turn. Many beaches and harbors are found along the shore. Warm subtropical waters bathe the northern shores, while cold currents wash up from the south. The ocean supports many kinds of fish, shellfish, and other marine life.

SOUTHERN HEMISPHERE SEASONS

Seasons are caused by the tilt of the earth on its axis, approximately 23.4 degrees from vertical. This tilt causes sunlight to hit the Northern Hemisphere more directly in May, June, and July. This results in summers for those living in North America, Europe, and much of Asia. But the tilt also means the Southern Hemisphere receives direct sunlight in different months: November, December, and January. As a result, countries in the Southern Hemisphere, including New Zealand, experience their summers in those months.

AVERAGE TEMPERATURE AND PRECIPITATION

Region (City)	Average January Temperature Minimum/Maximum	Average July Temperature Minimum/Maximum	Average Precipitation January/July
North Island - North (Auckland)	60/74°F (15/23°C)	45/58°F (7/15°C)	3.0/5.7 inches (7.5/14.6 cm)
North Island - South (Wellington)	56/69°F (13/20°C)	43/53°F (6/11°C)	2.8/5.4 inches (7.2/13.6 cm)
South Island (Christchurch)	54/73°F (12/23°C)	35/52°F (2/11°C)	1.7/3.1 inches (4.2/7.9 cm)[10]

CLIMATE

As a small island nation surrounded by ocean, New Zealand has a moderate climate. Summers are warm near the coast but not extremely hot. Winters are cool but rarely cold. Traveling inland brings winters that can be more severe.

Temperatures drop moving south along the islands. On North Island, summers are warm and moist and winters are cool and wet. Rainfall is high and spread throughout the year. Farther south, there are four distinct seasons. The weather here is known for changing abruptly.

Temperate, No Dry Season, Warm Summer

Whangarei

Hauraki Gulf

North Island

Auckland
Auckland Harbor

Bay of Plenty

Waikato

Tauranga

Hamilton

Whakatane

Lake Rotorua

Tasman Sea

Lake Taupo • Taupo

New Plymouth

Gisborne

Stratford

Napier *Hawke Bay*

Hastings

Palmerston North

Golden Bay

Cook Strait

Masterton

Karamea Bight Nelson

Richmond

Wairau

Blenheim

Wellington

Greymouth

PACIFIC OCEAN

South Island

Pegasus Bay

Christchurch

Canterbury Bight

NORTH
↑

Timaru

Oamaru

Lake Te Anau

Clutha

Chatham Island

Dunedin

Waitangi

Invercargill

Foveaux Strait

Stewart Island

Pitt Island

Climate of New Zealand

Two features exert a particular influence on New Zealand's weather: the ocean and the mountains. Warm subtropical waters bathe the islands, creating a warm and mild climate. Strong winds blow toward the islands from the west, picking up moisture and bringing rain to their western side. Fiordland and the West Coast region of South Island are among the wettest places on the planet. The mountains provide a barrier to the moist winds, making the eastern side of the islands drier.

CHAPTER 3

ANIMALS AND NATURE: SHAPED BY ISOLATION

New Zealand's varied landscape provides a home for a wide variety of plants and animals. Many are unlike those found anywhere else in the world.

Birds are the dominant land animals, and many of the native species are flightless. Many of New Zealand's birds are endangered, under threat from introduced predators and habitat destruction. One of these endangered birds is New Zealand's unofficial mascot, an odd but charming bird called the kiwi.

More than 60 animal species have become extinct since humans arrived in New Zealand.

The kiwi is a chicken-sized, flightless bird.

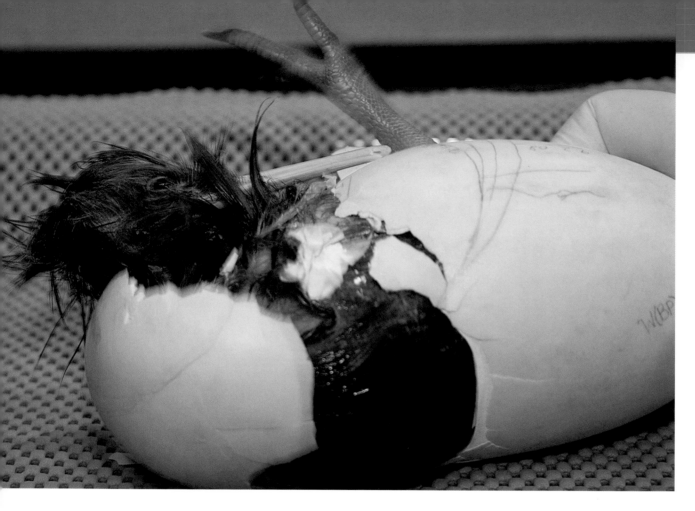

A kiwi chick hatches at a kiwi rescue center.

THE KIWI

The kiwi is a brown, fuzzy, flightless bird. These cousins of the emu have short legs, round bodies, and long beaks. Unique among birds, their beaks feature nostrils at the tip.

Kiwis at times seem mammal-like. Their feathers are loose and shaggy and look almost like fur. They sleep in burrows and emerge at night to eat, using their long bills and keen sense of smell to sniff out fruit and earthworms. They have catlike whiskers at the base of their beaks that help them sense where they are going at night.

The kiwi is unique to New Zealand. Like many of New Zealand's native birds, it evolved without land mammal predators and lost the ability to fly. Predators people brought to the island, particularly possums and weasels, have caused kiwi numbers to fall. There are five species of kiwi, and all are now threatened with extinction.[1]

The Department of Conservation has put into place a kiwi recovery program. The program includes efforts to remove predators from kiwi habitats. It also includes the Operation Nest Egg program, in which kiwi eggs and chicks are removed from the wild. The eggs are hatched and the chicks are raised in captivity. Once the birds are big enough to fend for themselves, they are released into the wild. The program has worked to help the beloved birds rebound. A chick raised in captivity has a 65 percent chance of surviving to adulthood, compared to just 5 percent for a chick in the wild.[2]

BORN OF ISOLATION

New Zealand's unique plants and animals are a result of the country's size and isolation. New Zealand broke off from the ancient supercontinent Gondwana approximately 80 million years ago. The islands' large area and

varied landscape—including high mountains, grassy plains, deep fjords, and wide beaches—provided different habitats for many unique plants and animals to evolve.

Some of New Zealand's animals evolved from ancient ancestors that were living in the area when New Zealand broke off from Gondwana. These include frogs, insects, and earthworms. Tuataras, lizard-like reptiles with spines along their necks, backs, and tails, are also descended from creatures that lived on Gondwana. Tuataras once lived on North and South Islands, but rats introduced to the islands hundreds of years ago killed them off. Now they can be found only on some of New Zealand's smaller islands, although biologists are attempting to introduce them back to the larger islands.

THE AUSTRALIAN BRUSHTAIL POSSUM

One of the biggest threats to native plants and animals in New Zealand is the Australian brushtail possum, introduced deliberately for the fur trade in 1837. There are approximately 70 million of these possums in New Zealand.[3] They destroy the habitats of native animals and eat the shoots and leaves of native plants. They also eat the eggs and chicks of kiwis and other native birds. To help control the possum population, people have taken advantage of the animal's luxuriant fur. Companies turn possum fur into hats, jackets, and bedspreads.

The ancestors of tuataras lived on the prehistoric supercontinent Gondwana.

Most of New Zealand's animals descended from ancestors that floated, flew, or swam to the islands after they had broken off from Gondwana. Many birds flew across the ocean, but the only land mammals to make their way to the islands were bats. Other land mammals found in New Zealand today were introduced by humans.

ANIMALS

New Zealand is home to some of the rarest animals in the world. The world's smallest dolphin, the Hector's dolphin, swims only in New Zealand's waters. An extremely rare sea lion known as the New Zealand sea lion also lives here. On South Island and Stewart Island, you can find the yellow-eyed penguin, the world's rarest penguin.

New Zealand is a land of birds. A third of

MOA

Moa were enormous flightless birds that lived in New Zealand until their extinction approximately 600 years ago. Scientists believe they became extinct only approximately 100 years after the Maori first arrived in New Zealand, a remarkably quick extinction. With their necks outstretched, the largest moa would have stood approximately 13 feet (4 m) tall, weighing more than 600 pounds (270 kg). However, experts believe the moa more likely kept its neck in a horizontal position, reaching up only to feed on tall plants.

The New Zealand sea lion is the world's rarest species of sea lion.

New Zealand's birds are either flightless or cannot fly well. They include the kakapo, the world's only flightless parrot, a shy bird that comes out only at night. Kakapos can climb trees by wedging their beaks into the crevices of trees and gripping with their toes. Like the kiwi, the kakapo is endangered and protected. Another flightless bird is the wrybill. It uses its unique beak, bent right at its end, to probe for insects under stones in streams. Giant birds called moa once roamed New Zealand, but they were apparently hunted to extinction only decades after humans arrived on the islands around 1300 CE.

Many animals live along New Zealand's coasts. Dolphins, orcas, pilot whales, and humpback whales swim offshore. Many kinds of seabirds, including gulls, terns, and long-necked birds known as shags, fly over the water. The sooty shearwater makes an annual migration of almost 40,000 miles (65,000 km), flying in a huge figure eight across the entire Pacific Ocean before returning to the New Zealand forest to nest.[4]

PLANTS AND FUNGI

New Zealand has approximately 5,800 species of fungi and 2,500 species of plants.[5] Eighty percent of New Zealand's trees, ferns, and flowering plants are found nowhere else in the world.[6] As with New Zealand's animals, these plants evolved for millions of years in isolation.

New Zealand was once a giant forest, but 75 percent of the forests have been burned or cut down in the 700 years since humans arrived.[7] Only pockets of forest, called the bush, remain. The bush is

A ponga frond unfurls.

an important part of life, and New Zealanders go there to hunt, fish, or tramp.

On North Island and in the lowlands of South Island are lush forests that look like jungles. Most of the trees are evergreen, with thick, shiny leaves. Lush ferns and a thick layer of moss carpet the floor. Tree ferns grow in the forests; the best known is the ponga, or silver fern, which has silvery undersides to its fronds. The ponga appears on the New

KAURI

Forests filled with huge kauri trees once covered large areas of New Zealand. Today, the largest kauri tree in the country can be found in Waipoua Forest on North Island. The tree is called Tane Mahuta, or "lord of the forest." It stands 167 feet (51 m) tall and has a girth of 45 feet (13.7 m). Tane Mahuta is estimated to be at least 1,500 years old, which means it was already 800 years old when the first humans arrived in New Zealand.

Zealand coat of arms. Tall trees called kauri also grow here and can live as long as 2,000 years. The tallest tree, a coniferous species called kahikatea, can reach 190 feet (60 m) in height.

Beech forests grow on South Island's ridges and mountaintops. Because these forests grow where the land is not suitable for farming, they are the largest remaining areas of the bush.

On the mountains above the bush, alpine plants such as mountain daisies and giant buttercups grow. These tough plants are able to survive in the harsh mountain environment. The alpine plants bloom in spring, beginning in the north and moving southward like a wave.

Some of New Zealand's plant species were introduced to the island by humans. The Monterey pine tree, native to California, was brought to New Zealand in 1859 and is now the country's largest source of timber. However, not all introduced plant species have been as beneficial to New Zealand. Gorse, a thorny evergreen shrub, was brought to New Zealand early in its European colonization. It has become an invasive species, spreading quickly and threatening native plants by blocking sunlight and sapping nutrients from the soil. The government has spent millions of dollars trying to control the growth of gorse.

ENVIRONMENTAL THREATS

Humans have had a huge impact on New Zealand's environment. Maori, and later Europeans, changed New Zealand's ecosystems and caused many of its animals and plants to become extinct.

When humans arrived in New Zealand, the islands' unique animals were vulnerable. Isolated from predators for millions of years, the animals had few defenses. People easily caught seals and the flightless moa. Within a few hundred years, the moa had become extinct, and seals had disappeared from the coasts. The Maori also brought with them *kiore*, or rats, which killed small animals. They burned fires to clear land for hunting, gradually changing the bush into grassland.

Europeans brought even faster changes to the islands. Sealers and whalers killed huge numbers of seals, sea lions, and whales. Settlers destroyed much of the remaining bush to clear land for farming and grazing. They turned wetlands into farms and brought weasels, ferrets, and cats, predators that found flightless birds easy to catch. They also brought grazing animals, including goats and deer. These animals changed the makeup of the forest.

The result of these actions has been deforestation, erosion, and loss of biodiversity, the number of different plants and animals. These

problems can reinforce one another, making the situation even worse. Most of the nation's forests have disappeared. Animal habitats have been lost, and deforestation has created problems with soil erosion. Tree roots normally hold the soil in place. When trees are removed, heavy rain washes the soil away, sweeping habitats along with it. Many of New Zealand's unique species have become extinct. Nonnative pests have also taken a huge toll on biodiversity. Biodiversity is higher on small offshore islands where exotic predators have never been introduced.

ENDANGERED SPECIES IN NEW ZEALAND

According to the International Union for Conservation of Nature (IUCN), New Zealand is home to the following numbers of species that are categorized by the organization as Critically Endangered, Endangered, or Vulnerable:

Mammals	9
Birds	70
Reptiles	13
Amphibians	4
Fishes	23
Mollusks	5
Other Invertebrates	10
Plants	21
Total	155[8]

Deforestation has destroyed habitats for plants and animals.

In the middle of the twentieth century, people began to realize how much humans were damaging the environment. In 1948, when the takahe, a bird long thought to be extinct, was found alive in Fiordland, people took notice. They began to understand the need to save animals from extinction. They also became aware that introduced predators were a big part of the problem and began to understand intervention was necessary to save more species from extinction. They also realized there were few native forests left and learned deforestation was causing soil erosion.

Today, New Zealanders are aware of the damage humans have done, and they are determined to protect what is left of their natural environment. The government is leading conservation efforts, and New Zealanders take part by planting trees, breeding endangered animals in captivity, controlling pests, and helping maintain parks.

NATIONAL PARKS AND RESERVES

Roughly a third of the country is now set aside for national parks and nature reserves.[9] New Zealand's 14 national parks are managed by the Department of Conservation. These are treasured wilderness areas that are maintained as closely as possible to their natural state. Native plants and animals are preserved, and if necessary, introduced plants and animals are removed.

New Zealand is trying to preserve such areas as the Clay Cliffs Scenic Reserve.

New Zealand also has 34 marine reserves, places where fish, seals, whales, dolphins, and seabirds can thrive. Additionally, the country recognizes more than 220 islands as wildlife sanctuaries.[10]

GOAT ISLAND BAY

New Zealand's first marine reserve was created at Goat Island Bay in 1975. Two square miles (5 sq km) of ocean were set aside to be kept free of fishing. Before the ban, much of Goat Island Bay was barren. Ten years after the ban went into effect, the ecosystem was flourishing. Today, 100,000 people per year visit the reserve, donning wet suits and plunging into the water to observe the fish.[11] Scientists come to study a marine ecosystem in its natural state. Fishers benefit because large numbers of fish spill into the surrounding waters.

Raoul Island is one of New Zealand's many nature reserves.

CHAPTER 4

HISTORY: A LAND APART

Archaeologists and other scientists believe the ancestors of the Maori were Polynesian people who arrived from Southeast Asia and Indonesia approximately 800 years ago. Polynesian sailors navigated to the islands, sailing in *wakas*, or large, double-hulled canoes, and following the stars, winds, and ocean currents.

The Polynesians brought food crops with them, including *kumara*, or sweet potatoes, as well as gourds, yams, and taro. The islands had a dozen species of moa and large sea mammals such as seals. All were unfamiliar with the dangers of human hunters. Thanks to the abundant and easy game, the early settlers spread fast, establishing settlements ranging from the top of North Island to the lower tip of South Island within 100 years.

Polynesian people came to New Zealand in large seagoing canoes.

As big game dwindled, the Maori turned to small game hunting, along with farming and fishing, to support themselves. As the human population grew, separate tribes developed. Resources grew scarce, and conflicts between tribes arose. The tribes built *pa*, or sophisticated fortifications. Remnants of these can still be seen around the country.

The Maori culture was rich. Though they lacked a written language, they had an extensive oral tradition. They told stories of Ranginui, the sky father, and Papatuanuku, the earth mother, who ruled over the various gods of land, forest, and sea. Regional cultures and dialects developed as tribes settled in far-flung regions of the islands.

JAMES COOK

James Cook was an explorer who came to New Zealand in 1769. He was a keen observer, and he promoted New Zealand as an ideal place to build a British colony. He also mapped the New Zealand coastline, claimed Australia for Britain, and fought in the French and Indian War (1754–1763) in North America. He was killed in Hawaii in 1779 after becoming embroiled in a religious dispute with the natives.

THE ARRIVAL OF EUROPEANS

Europeans first came to the islands approximately 400 years after the Maori. Dutch explorer Abel Tasman brought two ships into Golden Bay at the top of South Island on December 18, 1642. The explorers were searching for new lands and the precious metals they might contain. Maori approached the ships in two canoes to find out if the newcomers were friends or foes. In response, the Dutch blew trumpets and lowered a boat to take a party to the Maori canoes. The Maori attacked, killing four crew members. The Dutch ships sailed away and did not return. After hearing Tasman's tales, European explorers chose to stay away.

In 1769, British explorers under James Cook and French explorers under Jean de Surville made their way to the land of the Maori. This time the Europeans landed and explored the islands. Cook made three voyages to this part of

Captain James Cook was one of the first successful European explorers of New Zealand.

the Pacific from 1769 to 1777, developing a relationship of mutual respect with the Maori. By the early nineteenth century, the Maori called the newcomers Pakeha. The origin of the term is unknown.

Other Europeans soon came to New Zealand, many by way of Australia. Seal hunters, whalers, and merchants came to hunt off the coasts. Flax cutters and lumberjacks came to harvest the forests. Missionaries came to the islands too. By 1840, there were 2,000 permanent European settlers on the islands, which were administered by the United Kingdom as part of the Australian colony of New South Wales.[1] The mutual respect practiced by Cook was disrupted as the movement of settlers continued to threaten Maori lands.

The influx of Pakeha changed life for the Maori, who came to depend on goods the Europeans brought with them. Some European goods, such as pigs and potatoes, benefitted the Maori. Others, such as muskets, caused harm. The new weapons changed the nature of warfare between Maori tribes, and an estimated 20,000 Maori died during a series of internal battles known as the Musket Wars (1818–1836).[2] European diseases, such as influenza, whooping cough, and measles, also claimed Maori lives.

Missionaries also had a significant influence on Maori culture. They intended to bring Christianity to the islands but were at first unsuccessful in converting the Maori, who had their own beliefs and traditions. The missionaries did manage to teach European farming methods and introduce reading and writing, bringing about the development of a written Maori language. Missionary influence among the Maori grew, and the missionaries were instrumental in bringing about New Zealand's founding document, the Treaty of Waitangi.

TREATY AND WAR

In the 1830s, the British decided to take formal control of the islands. William Hobson was sent to be New Zealand's first governor. On February 5, 1840, he presented a treaty at a gathering of Maori in Waitangi. The treaty was taken all around the country and signed by many, though not all, Maori chiefs. With this treaty, the new country of New Zealand was born, becoming independent of New South Wales.

Right away, there were disagreements over what the Treaty of Waitangi meant. Britain said the treaty gave it sovereignty over New Zealand and gave Maori full equality as British subjects. But Maori understood the treaty differently. They believed

HONE HEKE

Hone Heke, the first Maori chief to sign the Treaty of Waitangi, was an influential leader. He later came to view the treaty as harmful to the Maori. He was a leading warrior, and he ordered the cutting down of the flagpole at the British settlement of Kororareka in 1844, aiming to show his disapproval of the government without harming British settlers. Over the coming months, the flagpole would be cut down and reerected three times. These actions led to skirmishes between the British troops and Maori in the north. The British won the battles, but Hone Heke was pardoned afterward. He retired and died a few years later of tuberculosis.

they would share authority with the British and be able to govern themselves locally.

After the treaty was signed, the government forced many Maori to sell their land at a low price. The Maori felt angry and cheated. Clashes known as the New Zealand Wars (1860–1872) broke out between the Maori and Pakeha. The Maori won some battles, including a resounding victory at the Battle of Puketakauere, but they were eventually overcome by greater European numbers and resources. The battles dwindled in the 1870s. Maori political power ebbed away, and the Maori withdrew from Europeans, living in isolated communities.

Other events also changed New Zealand dramatically between 1840 and 1900. After gold was discovered in 1861, miners rushed in, and the European population of the island rapidly increased. Railways, steamships, and the telegraph arrived, changing how people moved about and communicated.

One of the biggest changes was the transformation of the countryside. Europeans cleared the bush, seeking to remake the wilderness into something similar to their British homeland. They also wanted to make room for farms and pastures. As farming progressed, much of New Zealand's land changed from forest to farmland.

The Treaty of Waitangi led to European control of New Zealand.

In 1890, the Liberals, New Zealand's first organized political party, came to power. The government introduced old-age pensions, championed family farms, and passed laws protecting trade unions.

In 1893, New Zealand became the first country to give women the right to vote. These changes gave New Zealand a reputation among some as a laboratory for social ideas.

WOMEN'S RIGHTS

In 1893, New Zealand gave women the right to vote. A key figure in the women's suffrage movement was Kate Sheppard. She pressured politicians and newspaper editors, organizing a petition drive that gathered signatures from more than 30,000 women.[3]

Today, women play a prominent role in New Zealand public life. By the twenty-first century, the offices of prime minister, governor-general, and Speaker of the House of Representatives had all been held by women. Yet, as in most of the world's countries, inequalities still exist. Women are paid less than men on average. They are also more likely to be victims of sexual and domestic violence.

THE EARLY TWENTIETH CENTURY

During much of the twentieth century, the United Kingdom was New Zealand's main trading partner. The relationship dated back to 1882, when refrigerated cargoes of New Zealand food exports were first shipped to England. For decades after, New Zealand functioned as a farm for Britain. Many New Zealanders felt loyal to the British Empire, and the government was firmly pro-British. Children even learned British history and literature in school.

A view of a street in Napier,
New Zealand, in 1931.

In 1907, New Zealand ceased to be a British colony and became
a dominion instead. This was essentially a change only in name. New
Zealand would not become fully independent from Britain until 1947.

As part of the British Empire, New Zealand became involved in
World War I (1914–1918), and the new country landed on the world
stage in a big way. More than 100,000 Kiwi men served the Allied cause
with France and the United States, along with 550 women who served

as nurses.[4] But the war was very costly in terms of human life. More than 18,000 New Zealanders died, totaling approximately 8 percent of all men of military age in the country.[5]

After World War I, New Zealand was rocked by the Great Depression of the 1930s. Prices on farm exports dropped. Farmers lost income. People lost their jobs and their homes. Riots broke out on the streets of Auckland. In 1935, a new government was elected. To ease the suffering, the government put into place reforms such as housing programs and a 40-hour workweek.

When World War II (1939–1945) began, New Zealand again fought alongside the United Kingdom. Approximately 140,000 Kiwis joined the fighting in the Pacific, North Africa, and the Italian Peninsula.[6] Although fewer New Zealanders were

New Zealander troops were deployed in Egypt during World War II.

killed than in World War I, this war had a more direct impact on the country. Conflict with Japan led to the establishment of large camps of soldiers, the construction of emergency airfields throughout the country, and the fortification of the coast. As men left to fight in the war, large numbers of women were brought into the workforce. By 1943, almost one-third of factory workers were women.[7]

> Almost 3,600 men served in the Maori Battalion.

Kiwi troops seized key objectives at the Battle of El Alamein in North Africa in 1942, and the unit known as the Maori Battalion fought bravely at the Battle of Monte Cassino in central Italy, suffering heavy losses. During the war, tens of thousands of US soldiers were stationed in New Zealand. Originally sent to strengthen the small nation's defenses, they would use New Zealand as a staging area for military actions against the Japanese.

THE LATE TWENTIETH CENTURY

Following the Allied victory in World War II, New Zealand's farm products were in demand around the world. The nation became a well-developed welfare state, with programs for low-cost housing, pensions, health care, and benefits for families. As the economy boomed, new industries developed. It was during this period that New Zealand achieved independence from the United Kingdom. In 1931, the British Parliament had passed the Statute of Westminster, declaring its dominions were permitted to claim their independence and British law would no longer necessarily apply to them. New Zealand adopted the statute in 1947, making it an independent part of the Commonwealth.

Also during this time, immigrants flooded into the country, many of them from the United Kingdom. New Zealand's population became more urban as people moved to the largest cities. Similar to many other New Zealanders, Maori moved from the countryside to the cities in the 1960s, but they faced discrimination. Eventually, they began to speak up about their poor treatment in an organized way. Inspired by the civil rights movement in the United States, Maori grievances grew into a movement of visible protests. In 1975, a massive march occurred, a show of unity that forced the government to take Maori concerns seriously. That same year, the government set up the Waitangi Tribunal, a special commission to address Maori land grievances.

During the 1960s, 1970s, and 1980s, New Zealand's economy experienced many changes. The United Kingdom joined the European Economic Community (EEC) in 1973, a move that dramatically changed New Zealand's largest market for its goods. Members of the EEC were required to import most agricultural products from within Europe. Quotas reduced New Zealand's exports to Britain gradually until they were at a fraction of their former levels. Many New Zealanders felt betrayed by the United Kingdom. An oil crisis struck at almost the same time, hitting New Zealand hard. With its dependence on oil imports, the country struggled to pay its large oil bills. Optimism began to fade as inflation climbed.

Robert Muldoon met with US President Ronald Reagan in early 1984.

The economic instability brought about many political changes. In 1975, the socially progressive Labour government was ousted and a conservative National government came to power, led by Robert Muldoon. Muldoon set out to undo many of the economic initiatives of the previous government. With a Think Big slogan, he put forth energy and manufacturing projects of his own.

But voters came to dislike Muldoon's economic policies. In 1984, a Labour government was voted back into power. This government adopted an antinuclear foreign policy that strained its relationship with the United States. The government also took the economy in a new direction, removing government controls and changing New Zealand from one of the world's most regulated economies to one of the most deregulated.

In 1999, Labour leader Helen Clark became New Zealand's first elected female prime minister. The years that followed were prosperous, and the country had its lowest unemployment rates on record. In 2008, the Labour Party once again fell out of favor, and a National-led government was established under John Key. New Zealand entered the twenty-first century with forward-thinking policies, emphasizing clean energy production and protection of the environment.

ANTINUCLEAR POLICY

In the 1980s, New Zealand developed a policy of rejecting nuclear weapons within its borders. The United States tested the government's position in February 1985, sending the USS *Buchanan*, a destroyer capable of using nuclear weapons, to New Zealand. Since the US government had a policy of refusing to confirm or deny the presence of nuclear weapons on its ships, New Zealand authorities denied harbor access to the ship. New Zealand was officially declared a nuclear-free zone in 1987. In response, the US government suspended its military ties with New Zealand. Though the United States and New Zealand have since cooperated on some security matters, the ban on nuclear-equipped ships remains in place.

CHAPTER 5
PEOPLE: ABUNDANT DIVERSITY

As more people from overseas have moved to New Zealand, the country has become more diverse. In the past, most immigrants came from Europe, particularly Britain. British immigrants continue to move to New Zealand, but more recent immigrants also come from Tonga, Samoa, and other South Pacific islands, as well as China, India, South Africa, and other countries.

New Zealand's population hit 4 million in 2003 and reached 4.3 million by 2011.[1] Europeans make up the largest group of New Zealanders at almost 60 percent. Maori make up the second-largest group, with just over 7 percent of the total population. Asian peoples and Pacific Islanders each make up a significant slice of New Zealand's population at approximately 8 and 6 percent, respectively.[2]

New Zealand is a nation of growing diversity.

YOU SAY IT!

English	Maori
Good-bye (from a person leaving)	E noho ra (EHN ho rah)
Good-bye (from a person staying)	E haere ra (ay heye-ruh RAH)
Welcome, come in	Haere mai (HEYE-ruh meye)
Good morning	Morena (MOH-reh-nah)
Hello	Kia ora (kay OH-ruh)

LANGUAGES

New Zealand has two official languages, English and Maori. English is by far the most common language, spoken by approximately 91 percent of New Zealanders.[3]

The Maori language is a Polynesian language and shares its roots with other Pacific languages such as Hawaiian and Tahitian. Approximately a quarter of the Maori population in New Zealand speak it, along with approximately 30,000 non-Maori. In total, 4 percent of New Zealanders speak Maori.[4] However, many Maori words are part of everyday speech for other New Zealanders, and many place and street names are Maori. There has been renewed interest in the Maori language in recent years, and approximately half of those who speak it are under the age of 25.[5] After English and Maori, the most common language is Samoan, followed by French and Hindi.

MAORI LANGUAGE

Similar to English, the Maori language has five vowels. Unlike English, every vowel is pronounced, and every syllable of a word ends in a vowel sound. The language has only ten consonants, far fewer than the 21 found in English. Some aspects of English that involve adding or changing letters, such as creating plural nouns or changing verb tenses, are typically achieved only through context in Maori.

RELIGION

More than half of New Zealanders practice Christianity, and churches are prominent in New Zealand's cities and towns. The five largest denominations are Anglican, Roman Catholic, Presbyterian, Methodist, and Pentecostal. Jews have lived in New Zealand since the nineteenth century, and there are synagogues in many of the nation's towns and cities. Recent immigration has brought Hindus, Buddhists, and Muslims to New Zealand.

Maori religious customs and practices have their roots in Polynesia. The Maori traditionally recognized a number of gods and spiritual influences. There was a supreme god, but there were also gods related to specific things, such as earthquakes and agriculture. There were even tribal and family gods. Spiritual leaders conducted rituals and were said to be able to speak with the gods. Art and medicine were closely tied to Maori religious beliefs. Today, many Maori continue to practice indigenous religions, though they commonly draw on elements of Christianity due to the influence of early missionaries.

A Maori-created denomination of Christianity developed in the early twentieth century. Established by a Methodist Maori farmer, it was known as the Ratana Church. By 1925, as the new church developed its own rituals and hierarchies, Anglican leaders began to condemn it. The Ratana Church continued to increase its influence, becoming politically successful starting in the 1930s and eventually joining forces with the Labour Party. In the 1960s, the church reconnected with the other Christian churches in New Zealand and gained many white members.

Although religion played an important role in New Zealand's past, its role in society has declined, and the culture has grown increasingly secular. Among those who identify themselves as Christian, fewer than a quarter attend church regularly.[6] Many New Zealanders do not

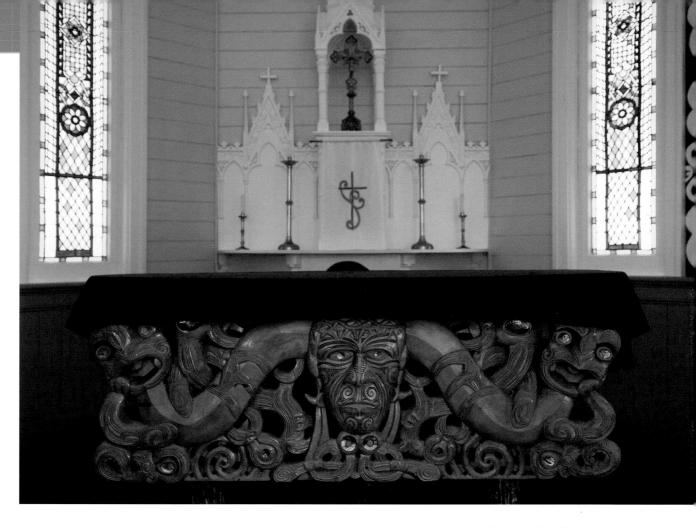

A Maori-style altar sits inside a
Catholic church.

participate in religious practice, and more than a third do not associate
themselves with any religion.[7] Yet within some populations, religion
remains important. Among those in Pacific Islander communities,
approximately 80 percent of people practice Christianity, and churches
remain at the center of community life.[8]

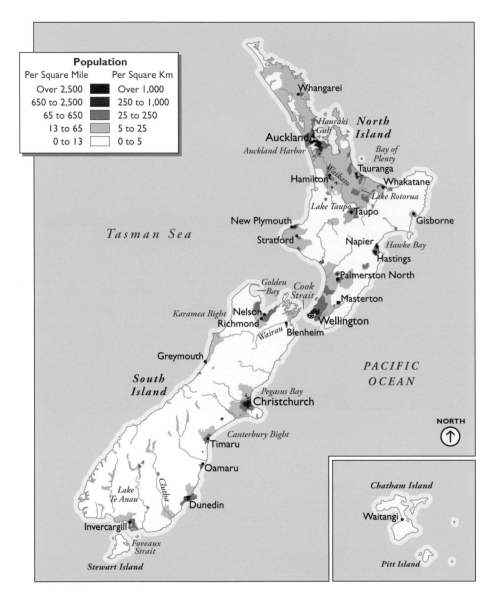

Population

Per Square Mile	Per Square Km
Over 2,500	Over 1,000
650 to 2,500	250 to 1,000
65 to 650	25 to 250
13 to 65	5 to 25
0 to 13	0 to 5

Whangarei

Hauraki Gulf • *North Island*

Auckland
Auckland Harbor

Bay of Plenty

Hamilton

Waikato

Tauranga

Whakatane

Lake Rotorua

Lake Taupo • Taupo

Gisborne

New Plymouth

Stratford

Napier

Hawke Bay

Hastings

Tasman Sea

Palmerston North

Golden Bay

Cook Strait

Masterton

Karamea Bight

Nelson

Richmond

Wairau

Wellington

Blenheim

Greymouth

PACIFIC OCEAN

South Island

Pegasus Bay

Christchurch

NORTH
↑

Canterbury Bight

Timaru

Oamaru

Lake Te Anau

Clutha

Dunedin

Invercargill

Foveaux Strait

Stewart Island

Chatham Island

Waitangi

Pitt Island

Population Density of New Zealand

AN URBAN NATION

Almost 90 percent of New Zealanders live in cities, making New Zealand one of the most urbanized countries in the world.[9] The largest city by far is Auckland, which has 1.36 million people. Wellington, the capital, and Christchurch, the largest city on South Island, each have almost 400,000 people.[10] Even people who live in rural areas are not necessarily remote, as many live near urban areas.

The twentieth century saw New Zealand's cities swell as people moved to urban areas. As immigrants moved from overseas, they largely settled in cities. Maori people also moved from the countryside to cities. Almost two-thirds of Maori now live in urban centers, although some still live in rural areas with their tribes.[11]

AUCKLAND

Auckland has a significant Polynesian population. Twelve percent of the population is Maori and another 13 percent are Pacific Islanders.[12] Many people live in close-knit communities where they speak their native languages. Some have formed clubs, getting together for traditional celebrations.

HEALTH AND LIVING STANDARDS

New Zealanders enjoy relatively good health. This is in part because of a mild climate, good nutrition, and a lack of big industries. Life expectancies continue to rise with advances in living standards, medicine, and health services.

However, Maori and Pacific Islanders do not fare as well as other New Zealanders. They have a lower life expectancy, lower standards of living, and poorer health. The life expectancy for a non-Maori newborn girl is 82.96 years, compared to 75.06 years for a Maori girl. A non-Maori newborn boy can expect to live 78.96 years, versus 70.36 years for a Maori boy.[13]

Diplomats receive a traditional Maori welcome. Though Maori have made strides, their standards of living are still below average.

CHAPTER 6

CULTURE: FROM TWO CULTURES TO MANY

At one time, the culture on the islands was entirely Maori. But with the large influx of Europeans, Western culture came to dominate the islands. Today, Maori culture is prominent and celebrated, but the mainstream culture is still European. As immigrants arrive from other parts of the world, particularly the Pacific Islands and Asia, New Zealand is changing from a bicultural society to a multicultural one.

Sports and the outdoors play a prominent part in New Zealand life. The country's traditions in food, literature, and art are blossoming, and new ethnic influences are changing New Zealand's culture in significant ways.

A favorite New Zealand dessert is hokeypokey ice cream, vanilla ice cream with toffee chunks.

Many New Zealanders are extremely passionate about rugby.

SPORTS AND OUTDOOR RECREATION

Rugby is a national passion and the most popular sport in New Zealand. Kiwis enjoy cheering on their national team, the All Blacks. The team is named for their original uniforms, which were completely black in order to distinguish the players from their white-suited English opponents.

When the All Blacks finally won the Rugby World Cup in 2011, people poured into the streets to celebrate. Other popular team sports include cricket and soccer.

New Zealanders enjoy playing sports as much as watching them. Sports and recreational activities are affordable and widely available for both children and adults. Some of the most popular activities are golf, tennis, and cricket. People also play touch rugby, and soccer is the most popular organized sport among young people.

HAKA AND THE ALL BLACKS

Before every rugby match, the All Blacks perform the *haka* dance. The players puff their chests, slap their thighs, and stomp their feet. They chant and poke out their tongues. The spectacle can stir up the crowd and unnerve opponents. Once, only Maori children watched and performed the war dance. Today the haka is a part of the renaissance in Maori culture, a slice of New Zealand culture that fills all Kiwis with pride.

New Zealanders also love spending time outdoors. Kiwis have a reputation as thrill seekers, yet one of the most popular activities is walking. More than 70 percent of New Zealanders walk for pleasure and fitness, and an extensive network of trails invites people to go tramping.[1] Some trails have an international reputation and attract thousands of visitors.

Many New Zealanders grow up fishing. Bicycling is popular too. In Auckland, many people enjoy sailing on the Hauraki Gulf. New Zealanders also enjoy swimming, surfing, canoeing, hunting, skiing, snowboarding, and horse trekking.

ARTS AND CRAFTS

The early Maori settlers brought carving techniques from their ancestral islands, and from these they developed a distinctive style of carving wood, bone, and stone. Artisans create designs with a type of jade called *pounamu*, also known as greenstone. Carvings are often in the form

of the *hei tiki*, a distorted human form. Among the most prized carved items are *waka huia*, intricately carved wooden boxes for storing family treasures. *Waka taua*, or war canoes, are also highly decorated with detailed carvings and are considered sacred.

Weaving and plaiting are the traditional crafts of Maori women. Long ago, they developed techniques for making flax fibers, reeds, or bird feathers into beautiful clothing, baskets, containers, and mats. Patterns are added to the weavings with dyes. Weaving and plaiting are once again popular, and traditionally woven war cloaks are still worn for ceremonial occasions.

Although the Maori lacked writing, weaving and carving allowed them to record their history and culture. History, tribal affairs, and stories were recorded through the intricate patterns in the carvings and weavings. In recent years, these art forms have gained attention from the outside world.

MUSIC AND DANCE

Live dance and music thrive in New Zealand's cities. Performances come in all flavors but remain uniquely Kiwi. Performers strive to take their music out of the cities to all parts of the country.

Pop and other modern music is popular in New Zealand. Local music often combines rock, hip-hop, or reggae with elements of Maori

Maori art is often based on the shape of a human head.

and Pacific music. New ethnic groups are adding their music to the mix. Popular musicians are found in many genres and include singer Bic Runga, Moana Maniapoto and her group the Tribe, and groups such as Split Enz, the Datsuns, Shihad, and Fat Freddy's Drop.

Maori have a rich tradition of singing and dancing. Men, including the national rugby team, perform the powerful haka war dance. Women perform the graceful *poi* dance. A traditional Maori performance art is the *kapa haka*, which combines the haka and poi dances with *waiata-a-ringa*, or action songs, and *waiata koroua*, or war chants. Kapa haka has undergone a revival in recent years. School, work, and tribal groups perform the dance at festivals and in competitions with one another.

LITERATURE AND FILM

New Zealand has a rich tradition of literature. Katherine Mansfield, one of New Zealand's most famous authors, wrote about New Zealand based on memories of her childhood. Recent prominent writers include poet Bill Manhire, novelists Patricia Grace, Keri Hulme, Maurice Gee, and Janet Frame, historian Michael King, and children's writer Margaret Mahy.

New Zealand's film industry is world class. It first gained international attention with Jane Campion's *The Piano* in 1993. More recently, the *Lord of the Rings* trilogy was filmed in New Zealand and

A man performs a traditional haka dance.

went on to win 17 Academy Awards.[3] In 2002, the critically acclaimed film *Whale Rider* was released. Directed by New Zealander Niki Caro and based on a book written by New Zealander Witi Ihimaera, the film received an Academy Award nomination for its part-Maori star, Keisha Castle-Hughes. Well-known New Zealanders working in film include directors Peter Jackson and Lee Tamahori and actors Russell Crowe, born in New Zealand but raised in Australia, and Anna Paquin, born in Canada but raised in New Zealand.

SIR APIRANA NGATA

Apirana Ngata (1874–1950) was an inspirational Maori leader honored in both the Maori and Pakeha cultures. The son of a powerful chief, he worked to develop Maori farming and improve Maori health. He helped form Maori battalions that served in both world wars and oversaw the building and restoration of carved Maori meetinghouses throughout the country. He also worked hard to save aspects of Maori culture such as arts and crafts, dance, song, and myths. King George V of the United Kingdom knighted Ngata in 1927.

FESTIVALS AND HOLIDAYS

Kiwis celebrate numerous festivals and holidays. Many observe the Christian holidays of Christmas, Good Friday, and Easter. Others welcome the holidays as a day off from work.

Waitangi Day is a national holiday on February 6 that commemorates the

Waitangi Day is a day of both celebration and protest.

1840 signing of the Treaty of Waitangi. Celebrations and events are held at Waitangi and around the country. Because the treaty is still controversial, some people use it as a day to protest.

ANZAC Day is celebrated on April 25. It originally marked the anniversary of the landing of ANZAC troops during World War I at Gallipoli, Turkey. Today, the day is used to honor all New Zealanders who have served in wars. At dawn, soldiers march to war memorials, and a parade follows later in the morning.

Holidays also help New Zealanders remember their historical ties to the United Kingdom. One day is set aside to celebrate the reigning monarch's birthday.

HOKITIKA WILDFOODS FESTIVAL

The Hokitika Wildfoods Festival is held in March each year on South Island. It has become famous for highlighting some of the most unusual foods in the world. The offerings include pesto ice cream, sheep eyes, possum pie, and worm sushi.

CUISINE

New Zealand's food has been influenced by European, Asian, Polynesian, and Maori cultures. The country is famous for producing high-quality meat and dairy, and New Zealanders eat a lot of both. Meats include lamb, beef, and venison. Dairy products include cheese, yogurt, and

Lamb is a popular dish for New Zealanders.

ice cream. New Zealanders also grow and eat a wide variety of fruits and vegetables. The most popular fruits are not native to New Zealand; they include kiwifruits, tamarillo, or tree tomatoes, and feijoa, a sweet, green fruit.

A traditional Maori food is kumara, or sweet potato, which the early Maori first brought to the islands. Other traditional foods include poultry and seafood. Maori have traditionally cooked food in a *hangi*, an oven in the ground. Men heat rocks in a fire and dig a pit out of the earth. They then place the hot stones inside the pit. Meanwhile, women prepare meat, fish, shellfish, and vegetables. The food is placed in baskets that are covered with wet cloth and set inside the pit. Earth is piled on top, and the food cooks slowly, developing a distinctive taste.

New Zealand's long coastline provides plenty of *kai moana*, or food from the sea, which plays a big part in both Pakeha and Maori cooking. Some favorites are oysters, mussels, lobster, red snapper, cod, and *hapuku*, or grouper. Many New Zealanders grow their own vegetables or seek out fresh produce at farmers' markets.

ARCHITECTURE

No one style of architecture dominates. Simple wooden houses sit alongside ornate public and commercial buildings and well-preserved Maori meetinghouses.

British immigrants often built in the style of the country they left behind. Over time, they adapted these styles to the New Zealand environment. Because wood was abundant, wooden houses are common. Public buildings were often built in the style of buildings in Britain. The Gothic Revival style seen in some public and commercial buildings includes arched windows, custom stonework, and towers.

Maori meetinghouses have gable roofs and feature elaborate carvings inside and out. The parts of the building represent the tribal ancestors: the gable symbolizes the head; the ridgepole, the backbone; and the rafters, the ribs. Another Maori design is the *whare*, a house

designed for protection against the cool climate. It is a rectangular building with a very small door. The roof and outer walls extend beyond the house to form a porch. Maori styles have inspired the design of other buildings in New Zealand.

ANS - TASMAN
SINESS CIRCLE

CHAPTER 7

POLITICS: A PARLIAMENTARY DEMOCRACY

New Zealand's government is a parliamentary democracy with a constitutional monarchy. The head of government is the prime minister, who deals with the day-to-day running of the government. The formal head of state is Queen Elizabeth II of the United Kingdom.

The government's power is distributed across three branches: Parliament, the executive, and the judiciary. New Zealand's constitution describes the powers and duties of each branch and how they work together. The constitution is not a single document. Instead, rules about how the government works are written in a series of legal documents. These include acts of the British and New Zealand Parliaments, as well as the Constitution Act of 1986.

John Key was elected prime minister in 2008.

For many years, two parties, National and Labour, controlled the government. In 1996, New Zealanders voted to change the way their leaders were elected, and they put into place a new system of voting. The result has been that Parliament is more representative of voters' wishes. Smaller political parties can make a difference and have their concerns heard.

THE HEAD OF STATE

Queen Elizabeth II is New Zealand's official head of state. She appoints a governor-general to be her representative in Parliament and to give advice to New Zealand's government.

The governor-general has official duties but little real power. Acting on behalf of the queen, the governor-general opens and dissolves sessions

STRUCTURE OF THE GOVERNMENT OF NEW ZEALAND

The Executive	Parliament	The Judiciary	Honorary
Prime Minister Executive Council Cabinet	House of Representatives	District Courts High Court Court of Appeal Supreme Court	Head of State (Monarch) Governor-General

of Parliament and conducts other largely ceremonial duties. In all but the most exceptional circumstances, the governor-general does not interfere in the day-to-day running of the government. He or she acts according to the advice of the New Zealand prime minister and the government in power. The system is known as a constitutional monarchy.

PARLIAMENT

New Zealand's elected representatives meet in Parliament to pass laws and approve government spending. The Parliament is unicameral, meaning it is made up of only one legislative body. New Zealand's Parliament consists of a popularly elected House of Representatives and the governor-general.

A session of Parliament begins after an election. The party that wins the most seats chooses a prime minister and forms a government. If no party gains a majority, two or more parties can combine to form a coalition. A government's term usually lasts for three years.

The highest elected official in Parliament, chosen by the House of Representatives at the start of each new session, is the Speaker of the House of Representatives. The Speaker presides over the House when it is in session and is supposed to act fairly on behalf of representatives of all parties.

The fiftieth session of the New Zealand Parliament began on December 21, 2011. Lockwood Smith of the National Party was elected

Speaker. At that time, eight parties made up Parliament. The two main parties were the National Party and the Labour Party. The National Party led the government, and the Labour Party was the opposition party. The other parties represented in Parliament were ACT New Zealand, the Green Party, the Mana Party, the Maori Party, New Zealand First, and United Future.

THE EXECUTIVE

The executive branch of the government is made up of the prime minister, the cabinet, and the Executive Council. The prime minister is an elected member of Parliament and the leader of the governing party or parties.

THE MAORI KING

Te Kingitanga, the Maori King movement, celebrated its one hundred fiftieth anniversary in 2008. It began in the 1850s, when a central concern was to retain Maori land and halt land sales. The Maori monarch has no legal status, but the symbolic position has significant prestige. The monarch is chosen by tribal leaders on the day of the previous monarch's funeral. Though there is no requirement that the monarchy pass through bloodlines, all Maori monarchs to date have been descendants of the first Maori king, Potatau Te Wherowhero. Yet there is always the possibility for the monarchy to be passed to another family or tribe if the tribal leaders agree. The current king, Tuheitia Paki, has served since 2006.

Parliament in Wellington, New Zealand

John Key became prime minister in November 2008 and remained in power after leading the National Party to victory in the 2011 elections. The prime minister's job is to appoint cabinet ministers, serve as the main spokesperson for the government, and give formal advice to the governor-general. Since the electoral system was reformed in 1996, prime ministers have had to lead coalition governments. These are governments made up of different political parties with different agendas.

The prime minister selects advisers known as ministers, who manage different departments in the government. All ministers are members of Parliament and together make up the cabinet. The cabinet and the prime minister together are commonly called "the government."

The executive branch also contains the Executive Council, which the governor-general presides over. It does not make policy decisions, but it gives formal advice to the governor-general.

THE JUDICIARY

The role of judges is to interpret the laws. The judiciary is separate from Parliament and the executive branch. Judges are appointed by the governor-general. Although the judiciary is independent of Parliament, judges cannot overturn laws Parliament makes.

A man casts his ballot in the November 2011 election.

A hierarchy of courts hears cases. Judges act as neutral referees while each side presents its case. There are special courts to rule on particular matters. These include courts to handle family and employment matters, environmental issues, and issues surrounding Maori land disputes.

ELECTORAL SYSTEM

All citizens and permanent residents aged 18 and older are eligible to vote for members of Parliament. Eligible voters must register to vote, although voting itself is not mandatory.

Under New Zealand's electoral system, each voter has two votes: an electoral vote and a party vote. The electoral vote is used to select a candidate running to represent the voter's region in Parliament. The party vote is for the political party the voter wants to see represented in Parliament. A party must score 5 percent or more of the total party

The flag of New Zealand

vote to gain a seat. Parties choose who they want to fill their seats, beginning with the winners of the electoral vote, then choosing people from their own list of candidates.

In 2008, the country was divided into 63 general seats, to be contested in the electoral vote. Seven additional seats were set aside for Maori representatives. After the votes were counted, another 52 seats in Parliament went to the political parties (resulting from the party vote), making a total of 122 seats in Parliament. The number of seats can vary slightly from election to election. The boundaries are redrawn every five years after each census, and the number of representatives can change as the population goes up or down.

The system represents an effort to keep the makeup of Parliament representative of the total electorate. Parties with at least 5 percent support are represented in Parliament. They can join other parties to form coalition governments and can have their concerns heard. Under this system, it is unlikely that a single party can gain a majority and form a government by itself.

LOCAL GOVERNMENT

Local authorities carry out some of the tasks of government. New Zealand has 11 regional councils, representing 11 of the country's 16 regions. There are also six unitary authorities, bodies that have a similar purpose. They handle public transportation and environmental issues such as plant and animal pests and river management.

There are also 67 smaller territorial authorities. They include 12 city councils, 54 district councils in rural areas, and the Auckland Council. The territorial authorities handle day-to-day local matters pertaining to issues such as recreation, water, sewage, local roads, and local land use.

CHAPTER 8

ECONOMICS: FARMING, TOURISM, AND TRADE

Once a mainly agricultural society, New Zealand has shifted in recent decades to a more industrialized economy. The island nation today thrives on a mix of farming, industry, and tourism.

New Zealand is an advocate for free trade. It depends heavily on trade with other countries and, similar to most nations, was affected by the global recession of 2008. Today, the economy is recovering, and unemployment is falling.

New Zealand has seven sheep for every person.

New Zealand exports sheep for both meat and wool.

FARMING

Farm exports have long been the basis of New Zealand's economy. Europeans brought sheep to the islands in 1834 and soon began exporting fine wool to Britain. In 1882, refrigerated shipping became possible, and New Zealand also began exporting meat, butter, and cheese to Britain. Today, the country exports farm products to more than 150 countries around the world.

Dairy and meat products are still New Zealand's largest exports. The main meats produced are lamb, mutton, and beef. New Zealand is also the world's largest exporter of farmed venison. Dairy products include milk powder, butter, and cheese.

THE NEW ZEALAND DOLLAR

New Zealand's currency today is the New Zealand dollar. Before the arrival of Europeans to the islands, the Maori did not use currency. When the British began colonizing New Zealand, they used coins brought from home. However, these were in short supply. Almost 50 different merchants began issuing their own copper tokens, featuring their business name. This practice continued until 1881. New Zealand soon began using British pounds as currency and then moved to New Zealand pounds in 1933. Under these systems, pounds were divided into 20 shillings, and shillings were divided into 12 pence. Seeking a less confusing system, New Zealand adopted the New Zealand dollar (divided into 100 cents, as in the United States) in 1967. Banknotes feature portraits of notable people from New Zealand's history on their fronts and images of the country's birds and landscapes on their backs.

New Zealand dollars

KIWIFRUIT

New Zealand is a major supplier of kiwifruits to the world. The kiwifruit has brown skin and a fuzzy outside texture. It must be peeled before it is eaten. The green flesh inside is juicy and tangy. Kiwifruits were brought from China to New Zealand in 1904 and were originally known as Chinese gooseberries. Then a New Zealand plant grower cultivated plants that kept longer for shipping. In the 1950s, the name was changed to kiwifruit, part of a marketing plan to sell more of the fruit overseas.

High-quality meat and dairy products are made possible by an abundance of good pastureland. Livestock are mainly grass fed. Grass growth fluctuates with the seasons, and farmers carefully time lambing and calving to take advantage of spring grass growth. Both North and South Islands have a mix of dairy, beef cattle, and sheep farms.

New Zealand's climate supports a wide range of agricultural products, including grains, wine, fruits, and vegetables. New Zealand also has abundant seafood. Top seafood products include squid, mussels, and *hoki*, a saltwater fish.

INDUSTRY AND NATURAL RESOURCES

New Zealand's chief industry is food processing. Another leading industry is plastics, particularly for food-product packaging. The country produces

A coal train hauls its load across the countryside. Coal is the most important fossil fuel in New Zealand.

fine wools and is a leader in the manufacture of textiles, carpet, footwear, and clothing. Other industries include telecommunications, forest products, electronics, climbing equipment, and luxury products such as yachts.

New Zealand's natural resources include coal, oil, gas, iron sand, hydroelectric power, gold, and limestone. Most of these products are used on the islands. Coal, oil, and gas help meet the nation's energy needs. Production of coal, the most abundant of New Zealand's fossil fuels, is centered around the Waikato region of North Island and the West Coast, Otago, and Southland regions of South Island. Iron sand, a type of sand containing high amounts of iron, is mined for production of steel. Limestone is mined for use in fertilizer, while gold is used in jewelry, computer chips, and electronics.

Another important natural resource is water. In the twentieth century, dams were constructed in New Zealand's rivers to harness the energy of the rushing water. The dams provide hydroelectric power to help meet the energy needs of the country. On the Waikato River and its tributaries sit eight state-owned hydroelectric stations. By 2007, hydroelectric power contributed 82.5 percent of New Zealand's renewable energy.[1]

TOURISM

Tourism is a booming industry. More than 2.4 million overseas travelers visit the island country every year.[2] Tourism employs almost 10 percent

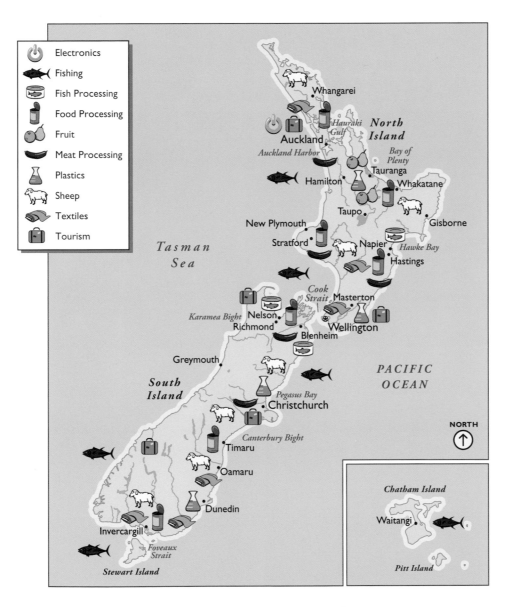

Legend

- ⏻ Electronics
- 🐟 Fishing
- 🥫 Fish Processing
- 🥫 Food Processing
- 🍑 Fruit
- 🍖 Meat Processing
- ⚗️ Plastics
- 🐑 Sheep
- 🧵 Textiles
- 💼 Tourism

Resources of New Zealand

of working New Zealanders, who find work in the hotel, food, and entertainment industries.[3]

New Zealand took off as a tourist destination after the world's first commercial bungee jump was set up near Queenstown in 1988. Other activities for thrill-seeking tourists soon popped up around the country. Today, there are opportunities for jet boating, skiing, rafting, paragliding, and skydiving. Ecotourism is also popular, featuring opportunities to see the country's wildlife and scenery.

Most tourists come from Australia, which sends more than 990,000 visitors every year.[4] The United Kingdom, the United States, and Asia also send many visitors. Tourists increasingly come from China, the fastest-growing tourist market.

INFRASTRUCTURE

New Zealand's narrow shape, mountainous terrain, and low population mean that communication and transport are key issues. New Zealand has always embraced technology that helps connect its people to each other and the rest of the world. An international cable system was completed in 1876, with telephone services following soon after. In the twentieth century came radio, then television, and finally the Internet. Even though

Tourists travel from all over to experience thrilling activities such as bungee jumping.

CHRISTCHURCH EARTHQUAKE

Earthquakes struck the city of Christchurch in September 2010 and again in February 2011. The 2011 earthquake was extreme. It caused 181 deaths, as well as damage to buildings, roads and bridges throughout the Canterbury region.[5]

The earthquake sent aftershocks through the economy and the labor market. Employment in the region fell by more than 8 percent for the year, compared to a national average increase of more than 3 percent.[6]

Christchurch is now rebuilding and has become one of New Zealand's fastest-changing cities. New restaurants, stores, and pubs are popping up. The city is planning an ambitious new city center, featuring low-rise buildings, green spaces, parks, and bikeways. Critics have warned that the reconstruction has become a drain on the nation's economy. Some citizens have given up on the city and moved elsewhere.

New Zealand is isolated, its people remain connected to the outside world.

Most New Zealanders travel by car. The New Zealand Transport Agency maintains highways, and city or district councils keep up the local roads. Airplanes are often used for travel between cities. The main airlines serving New Zealand's cities are Air New Zealand and Qantas. Commuter airlines link New Zealand's smaller towns. Ferry services link the North and South Islands as well as South Island and Stewart Island. People can also travel by rail, bus, or bicycle.

Roads in Wellington are often built through difficult terrain.

New Zealand's topography, natural disasters, and weather can make travel difficult. In Wellington, for instance, roads and railways must run along narrow valleys, limiting the number of routes and subjecting them to delays during rush hour. The transport system is also subject to earthquakes and bad weather.

LABOR AND EMPLOYMENT

New Zealand's labor force includes more than 2.3 million people.[7] Approximately 74 percent work in service jobs, which include jobs in government, businesses, offices, and stores, and 19 percent work in industry. The number of people who work in agriculture has fallen to 7 percent.[8]

New Zealand typically has a low rate of unemployment. From 2006 to 2010, during the global recession, New Zealand's unemployment rate rose from 3.8 percent to 6.5 percent.[9] The unemployed include those aged 15 years and up who are without work, are available to work, and are actively looking for work.

New Zealand's workforce has become diverse, as immigrants have moved to New Zealand from a wide range of countries. Yet not all people have benefitted from historically low unemployment. The

Former prime minister Helen Clark met with Chinese premier Wen Jiabao for free trade negotiations in 2006.

AUSTRALIA AND NEW ZEALAND

Australia is New Zealand's closest neighbor, its most important trading partner, and a key ally. Both governments are committed to cooperating on defense and have worked together closely on military matters.

The two countries have a shared history as British colonies. Many settlers came to New Zealand from Australia, but the two countries developed independently after New Zealand declined to join the Australian Federation formed in 1901.

New Zealand and Australia have many common elements in their cultures. They share the celebration of ANZAC Day, the anniversary of the 1915 landing of troops at Gallipoli. They also have many foods in common and are fierce rivals in sports.

New Zealanders and Australians can move freely back and forth across the Tasman Sea. More than 469,000 New Zealanders live in Australia and close to 1 million Australians visit New Zealand each year.[11]

unemployment rate is higher among Maori (13.3 percent) and Pacific Islanders (14.5 percent).[10]

FOREIGN TRADE

New Zealand relies heavily on overseas trade. For many years, New Zealand's main trading partner was the United Kingdom. Today, it is Australia. In 1983, Australia and New Zealand established the Closer Economic Relations Trade Agreement (CER), a comprehensive free trade agreement. Under this agreement, the two economies became integrated with no tariffs or restrictions limiting trade. The agreement also allows free movement of labor. Australians and

New Zealanders are able to travel and work in either country without special permits.

New Zealand trades with many other countries around the world. Trade with China and South Korea has grown. New Zealand also trades with other Asian nations, the European Union, and the United States.

New Zealand emphasizes free trade in the global marketplace. It strives to keep all markets open, negotiates with countries to gain market access, and works to lower trade barriers. The country is a member of the World Trade Organization and the Asia Pacific Economic Cooperation, an organization of Pacific Rim countries whose goal is to achieve free trade with no tariff barriers between its members.

CHAPTER 9
NEW ZEALAND TODAY

New Zealand ranked as the fifth-best country in which to live in the 2011 *United Nations Human Development Report.*[1] New Zealanders are well educated, healthy, and have a high standard of living. Extreme poverty and hunger are largely absent. Cities are not crowded but spacious and spread out like American suburbs.

New Zealand has a strong education system, and the literacy rate is high. Education is free and required for all children. Most children start school at age five. More students remain in school now than in the past, though Maori are more likely than non-Maori to drop out before age 18. New Zealand has a reputation as a leader in human rights, yet inequality remains, especially for Maori and other minority ethnic groups.

New Zealand's literacy rate is 99 percent.

New Zealander college students arrive at school.

NEW ZEALAND TEENS

Life in New Zealand is generally relaxed. Teens dress casually except at school, where uniforms are required. Families increasingly are a mix of ethnicities, particularly Maori, European, Asian, and Polynesian.

NEW ZEALAND'S NATIONAL ANTHEMS

As subjects of the British Empire, New Zealanders once sang "God Save the Queen." Today, the country has two national anthems: "God Save the Queen" and "God Defend New Zealand."

"God Defend New Zealand" was originally written as a poem by Thomas Bracken, who was born in Ireland. John J. Woods later set it to music. It became New Zealand's national hymn in 1940. In 1977, with the approval of Queen Elizabeth II, the New Zealand Parliament adopted it as a second national anthem. Today, "God Defend New Zealand" is often sung in both Maori and English.

School makes up a big part of teen life in New Zealand. There are four terms in the school year. Students get three two-week vacations in April, July, and October and a six-week summer vacation in December and January. The school day begins at 9:00 a.m. and ends at 3:00 or 3:30 p.m. Students learn from a national curriculum that includes English, languages, science,

Watching sports is a popular pastime of New Zealander students.

social sciences, technology, the arts, health and physical education, and mathematics and statistics.

Many teens work part-time jobs after school, and at home they do their share of the housework. They also listen to music, read magazines, play computer games, or watch television. Many have cell phones and computers and connect with friends by texting or on social media Web sites.

Sports and outdoor recreation are favorite activities for young New Zealanders. They like to play sports such as rugby, cricket, soccer, netball, and basketball. They love watching sports too, especially when the All Blacks rugby team plays.

Dinner is the main meal in a New Zealand household. Traditional meals include roast lamb, lamb chops, or steak. Kiwis also love to barbecue. On long summer days, they gather for casual meals in backyards, on boats, or on beaches. Traditional "barbie" food includes sausages and burgers, although thanks to the influences of many ethnicities, New Zealand food is becoming more diverse.

CURRENT ISSUES

The status of Maori and other ethnic groups is one big challenge facing New Zealand. The society is officially bicultural, and many New

Maori activist Tame Iti

KAITIAKITANGA

Maori believe everything in the environment is connected and interrelated. *Kaitiakitanga* is among their guiding principles. It means humans have a duty to guard and protect the environment for future generations. This protection also extends to human culture, art, and language.

Zealanders are proud of their country's stance on the rights of its indigenous people. Past grievances are addressed through the Waitangi Tribunal. Maori culture and language are celebrated. There are Maori radio stations, a television channel, and schools where children are taught in the Maori language. Maori have made gains in professions such as law, medicine, and business and are increasingly represented in Parliament.

Yet despite these successes, there is still progress to be made. Maori have a lower life expectancy and experience a higher frequency of major health problems, including diabetes, heart disease, and cancer. They have lower incomes and higher rates of unemployment. They are also overrepresented in prisons and have high crime levels and higher school dropout rates. Many Maori moved to cities during the twentieth century, and today, many are still poor and unemployed. A great deal more needs to be done if Maori are to achieve comparable status to Pakeha in New Zealand society.

The government's bicultural policy is a subject of debate in New Zealand. Some claim the government goes too far in promoting Maori culture, language, and rights; others claim it does not go far enough. Some people point out that New Zealand is home to people from many cultures, and they say the government should officially move from a bicultural policy to a multicultural one. They argue the country should officially recognize the cultures, languages, and rights of multiple cultures.

Another big issue facing New Zealanders is how best to protect their environment. Kiwis have a keen interest in the environment and conservation. They are

CLIMATE CHANGE

Scientists predict climate change will bring to New Zealand rising sea levels, increases in extreme weather, and increased pressure on natural ecosystems. This is likely to have far-reaching effects on New Zealand's economy. The country's agriculture, tourism, and hydropower all depend upon the stability of the environment.

The country has become a global advocate for policies that limit climate change. In 2008, it hosted World Environment Day with a theme focused on transitioning toward a low-carbon economy and lifestyle. It has ratified and implemented the Kyoto Protocol, along with other international agreements on climate change and the environment. The government has set goals to increase renewable energy production, expand forests, and research ways to reduce agricultural emissions.

Yet despite these efforts, New Zealand has the twelfth-highest rate of greenhouse gas emissions per capita.[2] Between 1990 and 2005, emissions rose 25 percent.[3] Agriculture contributes almost half of the country's total emissions.[4] This includes methane from sheep and cattle, as well as nitrous oxide from the breakdown of fertilizers and animal waste. Most of the remaining emissions are from energy production and transport.

scrutinizing their lifestyles, looking at how their choices affect the environment, and taking action to combat those effects. They are planting trees in erosion-prone areas, helping breed the takahe and other rare birds in captivity, and working to control pests such as rats, weasels, possums, and wild deer.

New Zealand's conservation efforts seem to be succeeding. The populations of takahe, kakapo, and other rare birds have recovered. Exotic pests have been removed from some small islands, and these islands have become sanctuaries for endangered animals. Safe areas have been created on the mainland using fences to keep out exotic predators. In 2000, the government launched the New Zealand Biodiversity Strategy with the aim of restoring natural habitats and increasing populations of native species. Since then, several specific goals of the program have been achieved, but authorities continue to work on broader, long-term issues.

NEW ZEALAND'S FUTURE

The twenty-first century promises to be an exciting time for New Zealand. Communication and transportation advances will increasingly allow the nation to compete in the global marketplace. The culture is blossoming, and new ethnic mixes are adding unique elements to New Zealand's food and music. Still, challenges lie ahead. As the country moves forward, it must work to sustain its prosperity, conserve its

New Zealand is trying to strike a balance between modern society and environmental awareness.

environment, and protect the rights of its increasingly diverse citizens. New Zealanders are a self-reliant and practical people who value human rights, tolerance, and environmental conservation. How New Zealanders meet these challenges will shape the future of this island nation.

New Zealand faces many challenges, but the nation's vibrant populace is poised to tackle them head-on.

TIMELINE

1200–1300 CE	Eastern Polynesian people discover and settle Aotearoa.
1642	Dutchman Abel Tasman sails to the West Coast of New Zealand on December 18.
1769	Englishman James Cook visits the islands and claims the land for Great Britain.
1818–1836	20,000 Maori die in the Musket Wars.
1840	The Treaty of Waitangi is signed on February 5 and New Zealand is proclaimed a British colony.
1860–1872	New Zealand Wars take place between Pakeha and Maori.
1861	Gold is discovered.
1893	New Zealand becomes the first country to give women the vote.
1907	New Zealand becomes a dominion of the British Empire.
1914–18	New Zealand fights in World War I with high loss of life.
1930s	Prosperity disappears as the Great Depression arrives.
1939–1945	New Zealand fights in World War II.

1947	New Zealand gives up dominion status and becomes a fully independent nation.
1960s	Mass migration of Maori to cities takes place.
1973	New Zealand struggles to cope with high oil prices and Britain's entry into the European Economic Community.
1975	Waitangi Tribunal is established to hear Maori land claims.
1983	New Zealand signs Closer Economic Relations agreement with Australia.
1985	New Zealand denies harbor access to the USS Buchanan in February.
1987	New Zealand becomes a nuclear-free zone.
1999	Helen Clark is elected New Zealand's first female prime minister.
2003	New Zealand's population reaches 4 million.
2008	Prime Minister John Key leads the National Party to victory in the November election.
2010–2011	Severe earthquakes cause widespread damage in Christchurch and the Canterbury region.
2011	New Zealand wins the Rugby World Cup.

FACTS AT YOUR FINGERTIPS

GEOGRAPHY

Official name: New Zealand (in Maori, Aotearoa)

Area: 103,363 square miles (267,710 sq km)

Climate: Temperate with sharp regional contrasts.

Highest elevation: Aoraki-Mount Cook, 12,316 feet (3,754 m) above sea level

Lowest elevation: Pacific Ocean, 0 feet (0 m) above sea level

Significant geographic features: Aoraki-Mount Cook

PEOPLE

Population (July 2012 est.): 4,327,944

Most populous city: Auckland

Ethnic groups: European, 56.8 percent; Asian, 8 percent; Maori, 7.4 percent; Pacific Islander, 4.6 percent; mixed, 9.7 percent; other, 13.5 percent

Percentage of residents living in urban areas: 86 percent

Life expectancy: 80.71 years at birth (world rank: 25)

Language(s): English, Maori

Religion(s): Protestantism, 38.6 percent; Roman Catholicism, 12.6 percent; Maori Christianity, 1.6 percent; Hinduism, 1.6 percent; Buddhism, 1.3 percent; other religions, 2.2 percent; none, 32.2 percent

GOVERNMENT AND ECONOMY

Government: parliamentary democracy

Capital: Wellington

Date of adoption of current constitution: January 1, 1987

Head of state: queen or king

Head of government: prime minister

Legislature: House of Representatives, commonly called Parliament

Currency: New Zealand dollar

Industries and natural resources: food processing, wood and paper products, textiles, machinery, transportation equipment, banking and insurance, tourism, and mining. Natural resources include natural gas, iron ore, sand, coal, timber, hydropower, gold, and limestone.

NATIONAL SYMBOLS

Holidays: Waitangi Day on February 6 celebrates the Treaty of Waitangi establishing British sovereignty over New Zealand. ANZAC Day on April 25 commemorates the anniversary of the landing of ANZAC troops during World War I at Gallipoli, Turkey.

Flag: Blue with the flag of the United Kingdom in the upper-left quadrant and four red five-pointed stars edged in white centered in the outer half of the flag. The stars represent the Southern Cross constellation.

National anthem: New Zealand has two national anthems with equal status: "God Defend New Zealand" and "God Save the Queen."

National animal: kiwi

KEY PEOPLE

James Cook (1728–1779) came to New Zealand in 1769 and promoted it as an ideal place to build a British colony.

Apirana Ngata (1874–1950) was an influential Maori politician who helped improve the lives of Maori people in New Zealand.

REGIONS AND TERRITORY OF NEW ZEALAND

Region; Capital

Auckland; Auckland

Bay of Plenty; Whakatane

Canterbury; Christchurch

Gisborne; Gisborne

Hawke's Bay; Napier

Manawatu-Wanganui; Palmerston North

Marlborough; Blenheim

Nelson; Nelson

Northland; Whangarei

Otago; Dunedin

Southland; Invercargill

Taranaki; Stratford

Tasman; Richmond

Waikato; Hamilton

Wellington; Wellington

West Coast; Greymouth

Territory

Chatham Islands

GLOSSARY

archipelago
> A group of islands or a stretch of sea containing many islands.

bush
> Native forests.

deforestation
> The clearing of forests from the land.

ecosystem
> A biological community made up of living organisms and their physical environment.

electorate
> All the people qualified to vote in an election.

erosion
> The wearing away of soil by wind, water, or other natural causes.

free trade
> International trade that is not subject to tariffs or other restrictions.

habitat
> The natural home of a particular plant, animal, or other organism.

hierarchy

A system in which groups are arranged according to rank.

Pakeha

A Maori term meaning people of European ancestry.

tariff

A tax or duty to be paid on imports or exports.

tectonic plates

Large, irregularly shaped, interlocking plates of solid rock that make up Earth's crust. The movement of these plates causes earthquakes and other geologic activity.

tramp

To hike or walk in the bush or rough country while carrying necessary food and equipment.

wetland

Land consisting of marshes or swamps.

ADDITIONAL RESOURCES

SELECTED BIBLIOGRAPHY

Kirkpatrick, Russell. *Bateman Contemporary Atlas New Zealand: The Shapes of Our Nation.* Auckland, NZ: David Bateman, 1999. Print.

"New Zealand." *Lonely Planet: New Zealand.* Lonely Planet, 4 Apr. 2012. Web. 28 Aug. 2012.

FURTHER READINGS

Auger, Timothy. *DK Eyewitness Travel: New Zealand.* London: Dorling Kindersley, 2010. Print.

Harper, Laura, Tony Mudd, and Paul Whitfield. *The Rough Guide to New Zealand.* London: Rough Guides, 2008. Print.

Montgomery, Sy, and Nic Bishop. *Kakapo Rescue: Saving the World's Strangest Parrot.* Boston: Houghton Mifflin, 2010. Print.

WEB LINKS

To learn more about New Zealand, visit ABDO Publishing Company online at **www.abdopublishing.com**. Web sites about New Zealand are featured on our Book Links page. These links are routinely monitored and updated to provide the most current information available.

PLACES TO VISIT

If you are ever in New Zealand, consider checking out these important and interesting sites!

Abel Tasman National Park

This is New Zealand's smallest but most visited national park. It is known for its golden beaches, abundant wildlife, and lush bushland.

Auckland

New Zealand's largest city is also the largest Polynesian city in the world.

Milford Sound

Fiordland's most famous attraction is best experienced by boat. The tallest peak is Mitre Peak, which rises 5,550 feet (1,692 m) out of the deep fiord.

Rotorua

This dynamic thermal area on North Island is home to hot springs, boiling mud pools, and beautiful Lake Rotorua. As 35 percent of the population is Maori, it is also known as the heartland of Maori culture.

SOURCE NOTES

CHAPTER 1. A VISIT TO NEW ZEALAND

1. "Legally Protected Conservation Land in New Zealand." *Ministry for the Environment*. Ministry for the Environment, Apr. 2012. Web. 27 Aug. 2012.

CHAPTER 2. GEOGRAPHY: VARIETY IN A SMALL SPACE

1. "The World Factbook: New Zealand." *Central Intelligence Agency*. Central Intelligence Agency, 15 Aug. 2012. Web. 8 Aug. 2012.

2. "Subnational Population Estimates." *Statistics New Zealand*. Statistics New Zealand, 30 June 2011. Web. 28 Aug. 2012.

3. "Environment Canterbury." *Local Government Online*. The New Zealand Local Government Internet Portal, 2010. Web. 28 Aug. 2012.

4. "Facts and Figures." *About Nelson*. Nelson City Council, 25 May 2012. Web. 28 Aug. 2012.

5. Carl Walrond. "Natural Environment - Geography and Geology." *Te Ara - The Encyclopedia of New Zealand*. New Zealand Ministry for Culture and Heritage, 2009. Web. 28 Aug. 2012.

6. Andy Dennis. "Mountains – North Island Mountains." *Te Ara - The Encyclopedia of New Zealand*. New Zealand Ministry for Culture and Heritage, 1 Mar. 2009. Web. 28 Aug. 2012.

7. Andy Dennis. "Mountains – South Island Mountains." *Te Ara - The Encyclopedia of New Zealand*. New Zealand Ministry for Culture and Heritage, 1 Mar. 2009. Web. 28 Aug. 2012.

8. "Stewart Island." *Encyclopædia Britannica*. Encyclopædia Britannica, 2012. Web. 28 Aug. 2012.

9. "Lake Taupo." *Encyclopædia Britannica*. Encyclopædia Britannica, 2012. Web. 28 Aug. 2012.

10. "New Zealand." *Weatherbase*. Canty and Associates, 2012. Web. 2 Aug. 2012.

CHAPTER 3. ANIMALS AND NATURE: SHAPED BY ISOLATION

1. "Operation Nest Egg." *BNZ Save the Kiwi*. BNZ Save the Kiwi Trust, n.d. Web. 27 Aug. 2012.

2. Ibid.

3. Gerard Hutching. "Possums in New Zealand." *Te Ara - The Encyclopedia of New Zealand*. New Zealand Ministry for Culture and Heritage, 1 Mar. 2009. Web. 28 Aug. 2012.

4. John Roach. "Longest Animal Migration Measured, Bird Flies More Than 40,000 Miles A Year." *National Geographic News.* National Geographic Society, 8 Aug. 2006. Web. 28 Aug. 2012.

5. Bob Brockie. "Native Plants and Animals – Overview - Species Unique to New Zealand." *Te Ara - The Encyclopedia of New Zealand.* New Zealand Ministry for Culture and Heritage, 2009. Web. 28 Aug. 2012.

6. Ibid.

7. "Pressures on the Land." *The State of Our Land.* Ministry for the Environment, 2012. Web. 28 Aug. 2012.

8. "Summary Statistics: Summaries by Country, Table 5, Threatened Species in Each Country." *IUCN Red List of Threatened Species.* International Union for Conservation of Nature and Natural Resources, 2011. Web. 28 Aug. 2012.

9. "Legally Protected Conservation Land in New Zealand." *Ministry for the Environment.* Ministry for the Environment, Apr. 2012. Web. 27 Aug. 2012.

10. "New Zealand's Offshore Islands." *Offshore Islands and Conservation.* Department of Conservation, n.d. Web. 28 Aug. 2012.

11. "Leigh and Goat Island." *Local Matters.* Local Matters, 2008. Web. 28 Aug. 2012.

CHAPTER 4. HISTORY: A LAND APART

1. "History." *Lonely Planet: New Zealand.* Lonely Planet, 2012. Web. 28 Aug. 2012.

2. Ibid.

3. Neill Atkinson. "Voting Rights." *Te Ara - The Encyclopedia of New Zealand.* New Zealand Ministry for Culture and Heritage, 17 July 2009. Web. 28 Aug. 2012.

4. "New Zealand and the First World War." *War and Society.* New Zealand History Online, 11 May 2012. Web. 28 Aug. 2012.

5. Ibid.

6. "New Zealand and the Second World War." *War and Society.* New Zealand History Online, 1 Sep. 2009. Web. 28 Aug. 2012.

7. Jeremy Black. *World War Two: A Military History.* New York: Routledge, 2003. Print. 259.

CHAPTER 5. PEOPLE: ABUNDANT DIVERSITY

1. "New Zealand Is Home To 3 Million People and 60 Million Sheep." *Statistics New Zealand.* Statistics New Zealand, 22 June 2012. Web. 28 Aug. 2012.

2. "The World Factbook: New Zealand." *Central Intelligence Agency*. Central Intelligence Agency, 15 Aug. 2012. Web. 28 Aug. 2012.

3. Ibid.

4. Ibid.

5. "Census Snapshot: Maori." *Statistics New Zealand*. Statistics New Zealand, Apr. 2002. Web. 28 Aug. 2012.

6. John Wilson. "Religion and the Churches." *Te Ara - The Encyclopedia of New Zealand*. New Zealand Ministry for Culture and Heritage, 3 July 2012. Web. 28 Aug. 2012.

7. "The World Factbook: New Zealand." *Central Intelligence Agency*. Central Intelligence Agency, 15 Aug. 2012. Web. 28 Aug. 2012.

8. "QuickStats About Pacific Peoples." *Statistics New Zealand*. Statistics New Zealand, 2006. Web. 28 Aug. 2012.

9. "The World Factbook: New Zealand." *Central Intelligence Agency*. Central Intelligence Agency, 15 Aug. 2012. Web. 28 Aug. 2012.

10. Ibid.

11. Te Ahukaramu Charles Royal. "People and Culture Today." Te Ara - The Encyclopedia of New Zealand. New Zealand Ministry for Culture and Heritage, 3 Mar. 2009. Web. 28 Aug. 2012.

12. "About Auckland." *The University of Auckland*. The University of Auckland, n.d. Web. 28 Aug. 2012.

13. "Period Life Tables." *Statistics New Zealand*. Statistics New Zealand, 2007. Web. 28 Aug. 2012.

CHAPTER 6. CULTURE: FROM TWO CULTURES TO MANY

1. Jock Phillips. "Sports and Leisure - Informal Sports." *Te Ara - The Encyclopedia of New Zealand*. New Zealand Ministry for Culture and Heritage, 2009. Web. 28 Aug. 2012.

2. "Te Araroa - The Long New Zealand Trail." *New Zealand.com*. NewZealand.com, 2012. Web. 28 Aug. 2012.

3. "Rings Scores Oscars Clean Sweep." *BBC News*. BBC News, 1 Mar. 2004. Web. 28 Aug. 2012.

CHAPTER 7. POLITICS: A PARLIAMENTARY DEMOCRACY

None.

CHAPTER 8. ECONOMICS: FARMING, TOURISM, AND TRADE

1. John E. Martin. "Hydroelectricity." *Te Ara - The Encyclopedia of New Zealand.* New Zealand Ministry for Culture and Heritage, 2011. Web. 28 Aug. 2012.

2. Margaret McClure. "Tourist Industry." *Te Ara - The Encyclopedia of New Zealand.* New Zealand Ministry for Culture and Heritage, 2011. Web. 28 Aug. 2012.

3. Ibid.

4. "Media Information: New Zealand." *New Zealand.com.* NewZealand.com, 2009. Web. 28 Aug. 2012.

5. Brett Atkinson. "Christchurch and Canterbury." *Lonely Planet: New Zealand.* Lonely Planet, 2012. Web. 28 Aug. 2012.

6. "Economic Effects of The Canterbury Earthquakes." *New Zealand Parliament.* New Zealand Parliament, Dec. 2011. Web. 28 Aug. 2012.

7. "The World Factbook: New Zealand." *Central Intelligence Agency.* Central Intelligence Agency, 15 Aug. 2012. Web. 8 Aug. 2012.

8. Ibid.

9. "Unemployment." *2010 Social Report.* Ministry of Social Development, 2010. Web. 28 Aug. 2012.

10. "Labor Market Factsheets." *Labor Market and Skills.* Ministry of Business, Innovation & Employment, June 2012. Web. 28 Aug. 2012.

11. "New Zealand Official Yearbook." *Statistics New Zealand.* Statistics New Zealand, 2008. Web. 28 Aug. 2012.

CHAPTER 9. NEW ZEALAND TODAY

1. "New Zealand Country Profile: Human Development Indicators." *International Human Development Indicators.* United Nations Development Programme, 2011. Web. 28 Aug. 2012.

2. Eric Pawson. "Economy and the Environment." *Te Ara - The Encyclopedia of New Zealand.* New Zealand Ministry for Culture and Heritage, 5 Mar. 2010. Web. 28 Aug. 2012.

3. Ibid.

4. Ibid.

[INDEX]

PHOTO CREDITS